LIGHT

by Anne Miranda

LIGHT

by Anne Miranda
Photographs courtesy of:
www.pixabay.com

First Digital Edition, 2021
ISBN: 9798588137478

Published by www.annemiranda.com

There's light every morning,

and light every night.

The moonlight is soft,

and the sunlight is bright.

A star lights our planet.

They twinkle in space.

Light makes things grow,

and it shines on your face.

Light bathes the desert,

and gleams in the plains.

Light dims when it's snowing,

and strikes when it rains.

It weaves through a canyon,

and glows in a cave.

It cuts through the trees,

and reflects on a wave.

There is light in a city,

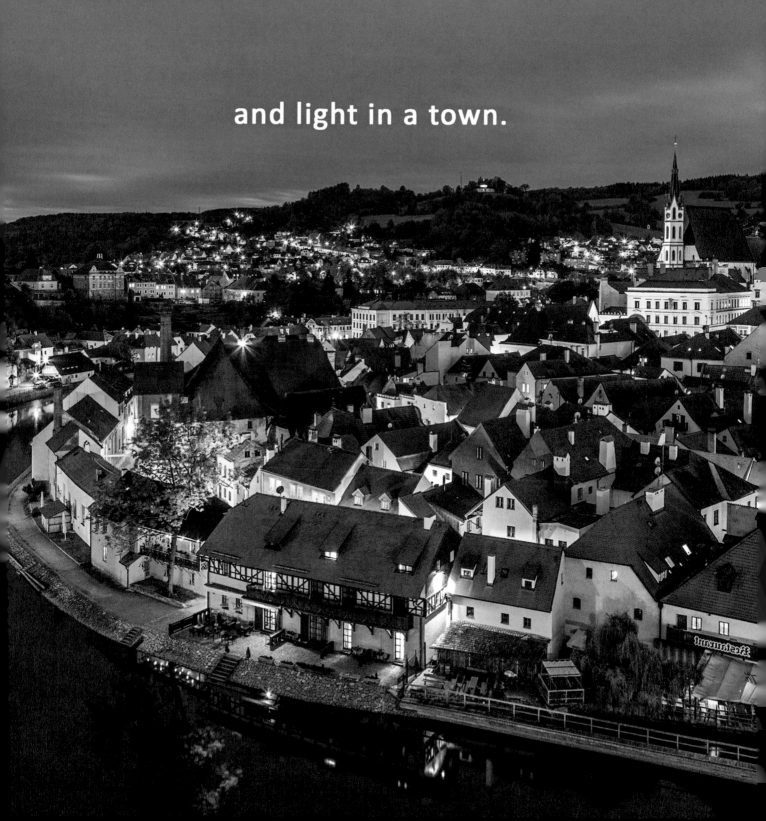

and light in a town.

There are colorful lights
that are blue, red and brown.

Light's warm like a fire.

It dazzles a lake.

Some lights are real.

and some others are fake.

Light is for animals,

people,

and plants,

lizards,

and jellyfish,

even for ants!

Light sends a message,

or sometimes a spark.

The smallest of beams,
can be seen in the dark.

Light lets us see!
What a glorious treasure!
The great gift of light,
is a joy without measure.

Book design by Tyler Miranda

Many thanks to the photographers on
www.pixabay.com for their beautiful images.

Made in the USA
Middletown, DE
18 October 2023